# Looking at Stars

# Night Sky

## Robin Kerrod

Belitha Press

First published in the UK in 2001 by
Belitha Press Limited, London House,
Great Eastern Wharf, Parkgate Road,
London SW11 4NQ

ISBN 1 84138 330 9

British Library Cataloguing in Publication Data
for this book is available from the British Library.

Printed in Hong Kong

10 9 8 7 6 5 4 3 2 1

Editor: Veronica Ross
Designer: Helen James
Illustrator: Chris Forsey
Consultant: Doug Millard
Picture researcher: Diana Morris

Photo credits
Robin Kerrod: 1, 14cl, 15bl, 18bl.
Lick Observatory, © UC Regents: 13cr.
Rob Matheson/Stockmarket/Corbis: 5c.
NASA/Spacecharts: 15br,
Royal Astronomical Society/Spacecharts: 10tl, 13bl,
Spacecharts: front cover, 7tr, 8bl, 8-9c, 9t, 9b, 11t, 11b, 13tl, 14br, 17c, 17b, 19tr, 21t.
Science & Society Picture Library: 17t.

# Contents

# Introducing the night sky

On every clear night, nature puts on a spectacular show – the starry sky. Thousands and thousands of **stars** shine down on our world out of the blackness that is space. They twinkle and sparkle like jewels scattered on black velvet. We often call the starry sky, the **heavens**.

The heavens are full of other delights besides the stars. The silvery Moon appears most nights, shining brilliantly. Some stars seem to wander around the sky. Others seem to be falling to Earth. Sometimes, what look like big stars with long, flowing tails come into view.

# Starting stargazing

Every night, millions of people look up at the night sky to see what is happening. Stargazing is one of the world's most popular pastimes. Scientists who study the night sky are called **astronomers**.

To begin stargazing, you need no equipment at all, just your eyes. Go somewhere that is very dark, away from the glare of street lights and car headlamps. Always go with an adult you know. Let your eyes get used to the dark before you start stargazing.

▽ Wrapping up
*On cold nights wear a thick sweater, anorak, scarf and woolly gloves. Thick socks and boots will keep your feet warm.*

◁ Star guide
*Using a planisphere like this, you can find which stars are on view on every night of the year.*

▷ **Trailing stars**

*Even with a simple camera
you can take pictures of
the night sky. The stars
make trails like this.*

▽ **Some like it hot**

*A hot chocolate or other drink
will help keep the cold out.
A snack also goes down well!*

◁ **Jot it down**

*Take a notebook and pencil
to jot down notes about
what you see and when.*

# Winter skies

The stars look brightest on cold, clear nights. Winter skies are best. A few pieces of equipment will help you get the most out of stargazing. Star maps and a planisphere will help you find your way around the sky. With a pair of binoculars, the heavens look even more spectacular.

# Stars in your eyes

The night sky is full of stars. Just using our eyes, we can see more than 2500 stars. Through binoculars, we can see thousands more. Through **telescopes**, astronomers can see millions upon millions.

When you first look at the sky, it seems to be the same everywhere. But if you look closely, you see that different parts of the sky look different.

△ **The Milky Way**
*A faint milk-white band of light arches across the night sky. We call it the **Milky Way**.*

△ **Beacon stars**
*Some stars stand out like beacons in the sky. The brightest star here is named Deneb.*

◁ Sparkling like jewels
*In some parts of the heavens,*
*stars cluster together.*

# Bright stars

Some parts of the sky
have more stars than others.
The stars are different too.
Some shine brightly like beacons,
while others glow feebly like glowworms.
Some stars are a brilliant blue-white,
while others are yellow, orange and
red. Most stars appear on their own,
but some have companions. A few
group together in clusters.

▽ Colourful clouds
*In places, great glowing clouds*
*of gas and dust appear*
*among the stars.*
*These are called*
***nebulas***.

9

◁ **Orion in the night sky**
*Orion is a bright constellation and is easy to spot.*

△ **Linking the stars**
*Linking up the bright stars in Orion gives us a pattern like this.*

# Patterns in the sky

The first thing you need to do when you go stargazing is to find your way about the sky. Look at the sky for a while. Some stars are brighter than others. In your imagination, try to join these stars together to form patterns. Look for these same patterns the next time you go stargazing. When you see them, you are beginning to find your way around the night sky. We call the patterns the stars make the **constellations**.

# Flying swans

Ancient astronomers saw the same constellations as we do today. They named the constellations after figures they thought the star patterns looked like.

For example, one star pattern looks like a flying swan; another is like a scorpion with its curved tail ready to sting. Here is a hunter, and there are twin boys. Only a few of the constellations really look like the figures they are named after.

△ **The mighty hunter**

*Ancient astronomers pictured Orion as a hunter. He has a club in his right hand, ready to strike a blow.*

▷ **Fanciful figures**

*Heroes and heroines, beasts and birds appear in this ancient map of constellations.*

# Queen of the night

The Moon circles the Earth once a month. It does not give out any light of its own. We see it shine because it is lit by the Sun.

But the Moon does not stay the same every night. On some nights we see it as a thin curve, or crescent. On others it appears to be a full circle. On some nights we can't see it at all.

The Moon appears to change shape because different amounts of it are lit up by the Sun each night. These shapes are called the **phases of the Moon**.

## Turning round

*These pictures show different phases of the Moon. To get the right view, you need to turn the book round. Begin by turning it to the right so that '1 New moon' appears the right-way up.*

▽1 New moon
*At the start of each month, we can't see the Moon. This is called a New moon. The Sun lights up the Moon's far side. The near side, the side that faces us, is in darkness. (Turn the book to the right.)*

*(Turn the book to the right.)*
*darkness.*
*side is still in*
*Moon. The left-hand*
*hand side of the*
*lights up the right-*
*quarter. The Sun*
*call this the First*
*as a half-circle. We*
*the Moon appears*
*After about a week,*
▷ 2 First quarter

### ◁ 4 Last quarter

*After another week, the Moon again appears as a half-circle. We call this the Last quarter. The Sun now lights up only the left-hand side of the Moon. Over the next week, the lit-up area shrinks until it disappears completely at the next New moon.*

### △ 3 Full moon

*After another week, the Moon appears as a full circle. We call it a Full moon. The Sun is behind us and lights up the whole of the near side of the Moon. Now the far side is dark. (Turn the book to the right.)*

# Stars that wander

On some evenings, just after the Sun has set, a bright star appears in the sky. No other stars are out yet. We call this bright star the evening star. But the evening star is not a star at all. It is a **planet**. A star is a great ball of very hot gas like the Sun. But the evening star is a ball of rock, like the Earth.

▽ Rocky planet

*Venus is covered with
huge volcanoes.*

△ Evening star

*The evening star, Venus,
and a crescent Moon
appear together at sunset.*

14

# Circling in space

The evening star is the planet Venus. It is one of five planets we can see in the sky. The other planets we can see are Mercury, Mars, Jupiter and Saturn. Mercury and Mars are rocky planets like Venus. But Jupiter and Saturn are great balls of cold gas and liquid.

The word planet means wanderer, because planets look like stars that wander across the sky.

The Earth is also a planet. Another three planets, Uranus, Neptune and Pluto, are too far away to be seen. All the planets, including the Earth, circle in space around the Sun.

▽ **Great gas ball**
*Seen close-up, giant Jupiter is covered with bands of coloured clouds.*

▽ **Bright shiners**
*Mars (left) and Jupiter shine brightly in the evening sky.*

# Catch a falling star

When you go stargazing, you will almost always see bright streaks in the sky. It looks as if some of the stars are dropping out of the heavens or shooting off to a different constellation. We call these streaks falling stars or **shooting stars**.

But stars don't fall from the sky or move around. The streaks are made by specks of rock from outer space travelling through the air high above the Earth. They are called **meteors**.

▷ It's raining meteors
*Specks and lumps from outer space rain down on the Earth all the time. Most burn up in the air, but some reach the ground and dig out craters.*

▷ Metal meteorite

*This meteorite is made up of metals, mainly iron and nickel. But most meteorites are made up of rock.*

▷ What a shower

*Two meteors flash by during a meteor shower. In a shower many more meteors occur than usual.*

# Fiery trails

As the specks of rock hit the air, they heat up and catch fire. They leave behind a fiery trail that we see as a meteor.

Sometimes bigger lumps of rock don't completely burn up. Some bits fall down and hit the Earth. We call them meteorites.

Big meteorites hit the ground very hard and dig out craters. If a big meteorite crashed into a city, it would knock down buildings and kill many people.

▷ Meteor crater

*About 50 000 years ago a big meteorite dug out this huge crater in Arizona, USA. It is more than 1200 metres across.*

# Stars with tails

**Comets** are the most spectacular of the heavenly bodies. They can shine more brightly than the brightest stars. And their tails can stretch for millions of kilometres.

Comets circle the Sun, just like the planets. But they can take thousands of years to make the journey. Usually we don't know when they are going to appear in the sky.

Long ago people were afraid when a comet appeared. They thought it would cause disasters and wars. A comet appeared at the Battle of Hastings in 1066, when the English King Harold was killed.

The 1066 comet has been seen many times. It is named Halley's comet after the English astronomer Edmond Halley. It last appeared in 1986, and should return in 2062.

◁ **The comet of 1997**
*This comet was named Hale-Bopp after the two astronomers who discovered it. It was one of the brightest comets of recent years.*

*Jets of gas shoot out of the body of Halley's comet. A spacecraft called Giotto took this picture in 1986.*

# Ice and dust

Comets are often called dirty snowballs because they are made up of ice and dust. Most of the time they are frozen solid. But they start to melt when they are near the Sun. Then they give off clouds of gas and dust that shine in the sunlight.

△ Heads and tails

*The brightest part of a comet is the head. One or two tails grow out from the head as the comet gets nearer the Sun.*

# The heavens above

When we look up at the night sky, it seems like a great dark bowl over our heads. It is the same wherever we go on Earth.

Ancient astronomers believed that the Earth lay inside a dark ball, or sphere. They called it the **celestial** (heavenly) **sphere**. They thought that the stars were stuck on the inside of the sphere. They could see that the sphere spun round, and they believed that this made the stars move across the sky during the night.

We now know that there is no such thing as a celestial sphere. The stars are scattered at different distances throughout space. And the stars move across the night sky because the Earth is spinning round.

Horizon

◁ **The sky dome**
*Everywhere you go, the sky seems to form a huge bowl over your head. The bowl meets the ground in the distance, on the horizon.*

20

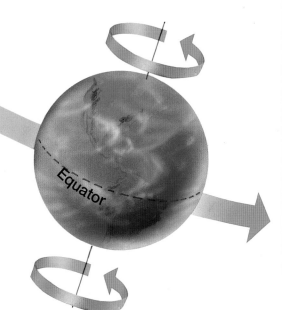

## △ Spinning round

*The Earth spins round in space once a day.*

## △ Star trails

*The spinning of the Earth makes the stars appear to whirl round at night.*

## ▷ The celestial sphere

*Astronomers once thought that the stars were stuck to the inside of a sphere that spins round the Earth. We can think of it in two halves, called the northern and southern hemispheres.*

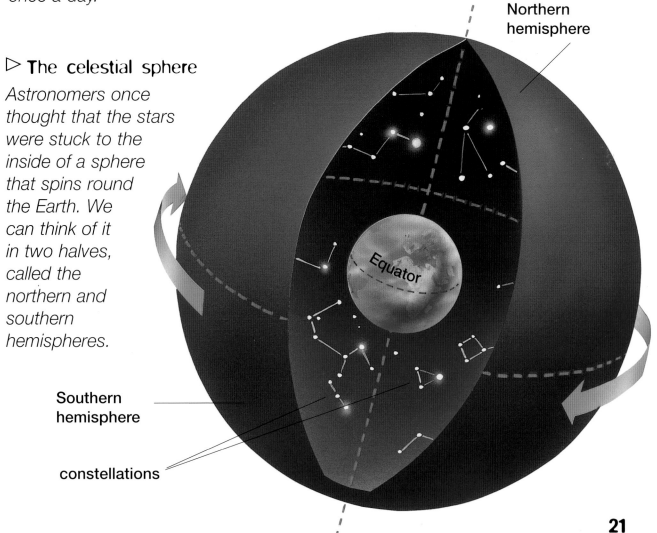

Northern hemisphere

Southern hemisphere

constellations

# Constellations north and south

Here are the main star patterns, or constellations, that we can see in the two hemispheres (halves) of the night sky. We show just a few bright stars for each constellation.

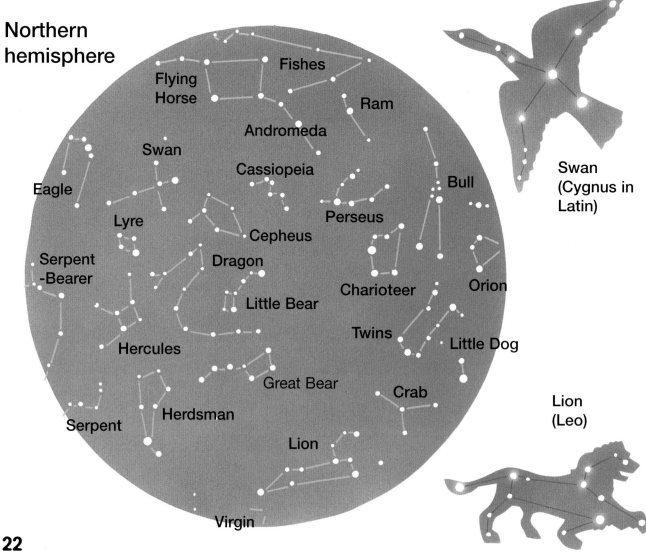

Northern hemisphere

Fishes
Flying Horse
Ram
Andromeda
Swan
Cassiopeia
Bull
Eagle
Perseus
Lyre
Cepheus
Serpent-Bearer
Dragon
Charioteer
Orion
Little Bear
Twins
Little Dog
Hercules
Great Bear
Crab
Herdsman
Serpent
Lion
Virgin

Swan (Cygnus in Latin)

Lion (Leo)

The names of the constellations are given in English. Astronomers give them Latin names.

**Southern hemisphere**

Scorpion (Scorpius)

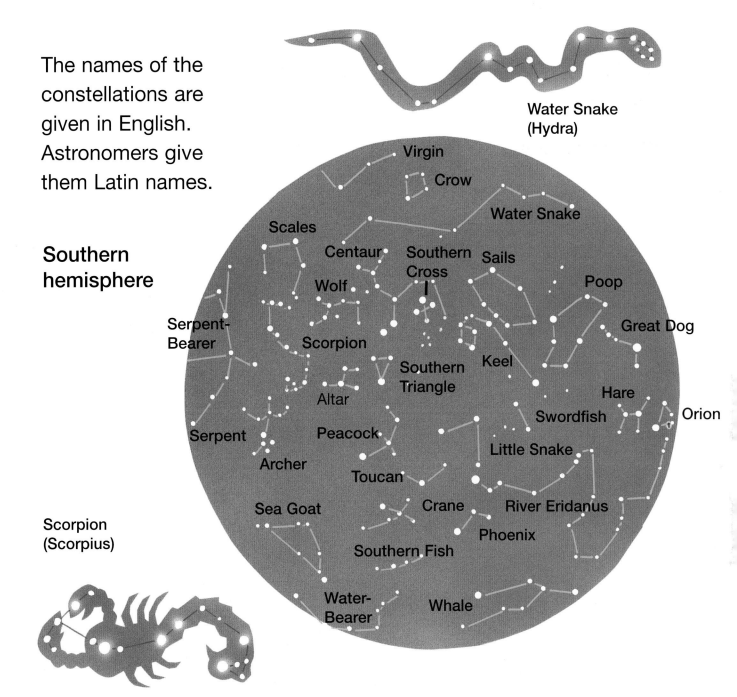

Water Snake (Hydra)

Virgin
Crow
Water Snake
Scales
Centaur
Southern Cross
Sails
Poop
Wolf
Great Dog
Serpent-Bearer
Scorpion
Southern Triangle
Keel
Hare
Altar
Swordfish
Orion
Serpent
Peacock
Little Snake
Archer
Toucan
Sea Goat
Crane
River Eridanus
Phoenix
Southern Fish
Water-Bearer
Whale

# Seeing stars

Which constellations you see during the year depends on where in the world you live. From most places you will see some of the constellations of the northern hemisphere and some of the southern hemisphere. But there are some constellations that you will never see. They lie on the other side of the Earth.

# Now you see them

The night sky never stays the same. It changes hour by hour during the night. And it also changes month by month and season by season.

When you stargaze for a long time, you notice that the constellations slowly move across the sky. This happens because the Earth spins round in space once a day.

The Earth spins round from west to east. This makes the stars move in the opposite direction, from east to west. This is the same direction in which the Sun travels across the sky during the daytime.

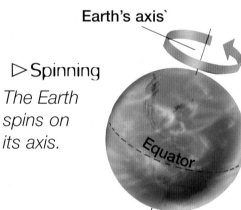

▷ Spinning
*The Earth spins on its axis.*

◁ Rising and setting
*The stars rise in the east when it gets dark. They climb to their highest point in the south. Then they set in the west when daylight comes again.*

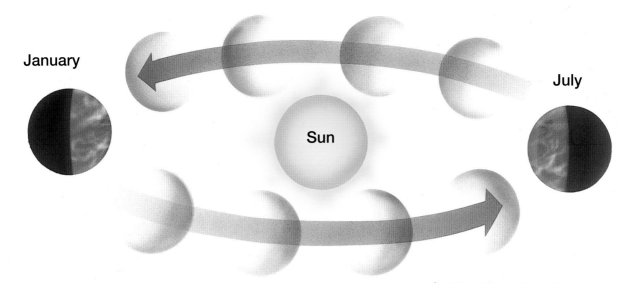

January

July

Sun

Because the stars are always moving, they lie in different directions in the sky at different times. This is why a time (10.30 pm) is given with the star maps that follow. The maps show the positions of the constellations at that time.

As the months go by, some constellations disappear and others take their place. The constellations change because the Earth circles around the Sun during the year.

△ Circling the Sun
*In January and July, the Earth lies on opposite sides of the Sun.*

▽ Changing skies
*In January, the night side of the Earth looks out on to one part of the heavens. In July, it looks out on to the other part. This is why we see different constellations during these months.*

January

July

Sun

West          North          East

# January skies

The maps on these pages show the stars you can see early in January. You see different constellations in different parts of the world. In northern parts it is winter. In southern parts it is summer.

△ **Europe, North America**
*Looking north at about 10.30 pm in the first week in January.*

▽ **Australia, South America**
*Looking north at about 10.30 pm in the first week in January.*

West          North          East

Twins

Orion

Bull

Little Dog

Fishes

Water Snake · Sirius

Lion

Whale

River Eridanus

Great Dog

Great Dog

| East | South | West |

In northern parts looking north, the easiest stars to spot are the Plough and Cassiopeia. Looking south, you can't miss Orion and the very bright star Sirius.

△ **Europe, North America**

*Looking south at about 10.30 pm in the first week in January.*

In southern parts, you find Orion when you look north, with the Bull (Taurus) and the Twins (Gemini) nearby. Looking south, you can't mistake the Southern Cross (Crux).

▽ **Australia, South America**

*Looking south at about 10.30 pm in the first week in January.*

| East | South | West |

Keel

River Eridanus

Little Snake

Sails

Phoenix

Toucan

Southern Cross

Centaur

Peacock

Crane

Whale

Southern Triangle

Southern Fish

Crow

West          North          East

# July skies

Here are the constellations you can see early in July. Now it is summer in northern parts of the world, and winter in southern parts. Many new constellations have come into view. Others have moved.

△ **Europe, North America**
*Looking north at about 10.30 pm in the first week in July.*

▽ **Australia, South America**
*Looking north at about 10.30 pm in the first week in July.*

West          North          East

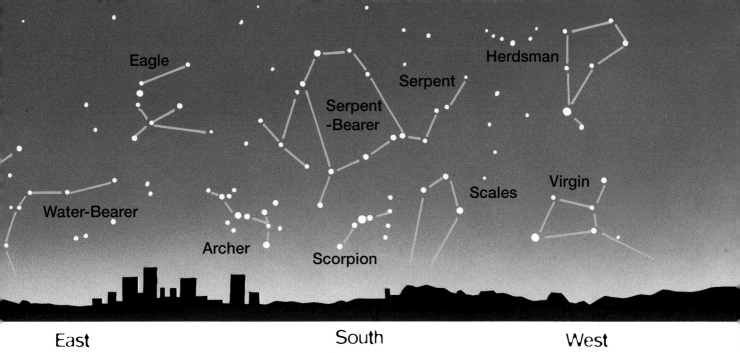

East        South        West

In northern parts looking north, the Plough and Cassiopeia have swapped places. Looking south, Orion has disappeared. The Eagle (Aquila) is easiest to spot.

In southern parts, the Eagle is found looking north, with the Swan (Cygnus) nearby. Looking south, the Southern Cross is now on the other side of the sky.

△ **Europe, North America**

*Looking south at about 10.30 pm in the first week in July.*

▽ **Australia, South America**

*Looking south at about 10.30 pm in the first week in July.*

East        South        West

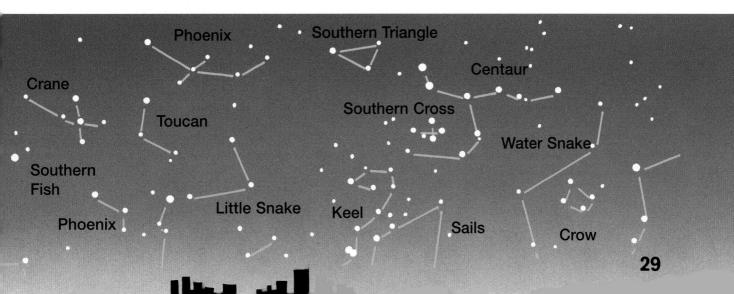

# Written in the stars

During the year the Earth circles around the Sun. But, seen from the Earth, the Sun seems to move among the stars. Every month it travels through one of the constellations. All the planets travel through these same 12 constellations too.

These constellations are known as the constellations of the zodiac. The word zodiac means 'circle of animals'. This is because most of the constellations are named after animals, such as Aries (the Ram) and Pisces (the Fishes).

People once thought that the constellations of the zodiac must be very special. They believed that these stars somehow affected what they were like and what happened to them. Even today some people think that the stars affect their lives. This idea is called **astrology**.

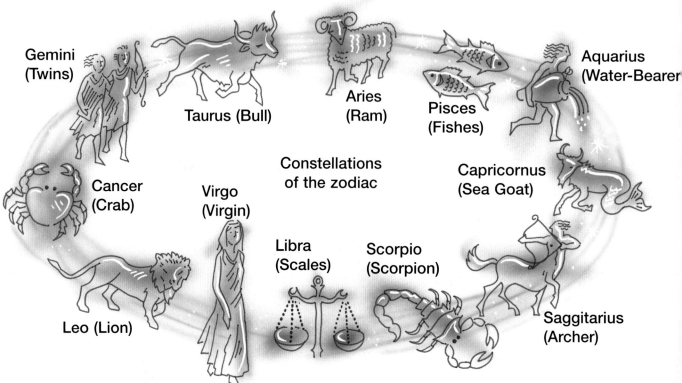

Gemini (Twins)

Taurus (Bull)

Aries (Ram)

Pisces (Fishes)

Aquarius (Water-Bearer)

Cancer (Crab)

Virgo (Virgin)

Constellations of the zodiac

Capricornus (Sea Goat)

Libra (Scales)

Scorpio (Scorpion)

Leo (Lion)

Saggitarius (Archer)

# Useful words

**astrology**   The idea that people's lives are affected by the planets and the stars.

**astronomer**   A person who studies the stars and the other heavenly bodies.

**celestial sphere**   The dark dome of the night sky, which seems to surround the Earth.

**comet**   An icy lump that starts to glow when it nears the Sun.

**constellation**   A pattern of bright stars in the night sky.

**heavens**   A name for the night sky. Heavenly bodies are the objects that appear in the sky.

**meteor**   A bright streak made when a speck of rock or metal burns up in the air.

**Milky Way**   A faint band of light seen arching across the night sky.

**nebula**   A big cloud of gas and dust in space.

**phases of the Moon**   The changing shapes of the Moon during the month.

**planet**   A large body that circles in space around the Sun.

**shooting star**   A popular name for a meteor.

**star**   A huge ball of very hot gases, which gives off heat and light.

**telescope**   An instrument astronomers use to gather light from the stars.

# Index